Under a MAUI SUN

AN ISLAND TREASURES BOOK

CHERYL CHEE TSUTSUMI
photographs by
RON DAHLQUIST

ISLAND HERITAGE
PUBLISHING

Under a MAUI SUN

THE VALLEY ISLAND

Published and distributed by
ISLAND HERITAGE PUBLISHING

ISBN 0-89610-394-3

Address orders and correspondence to:

ISLAND HERITAGE
P U B L I S H I N G
94-411 Kō'aki Street
Waipahu, Hawai'i 96797
Telephone 800-468-2800
          808-564-8800
www.islandheritage.com

Printed in Hong Kong
First edition, second printing, 2001

CREDITS: The photograph of the whale that
appears on the jacket is by J. D. Watt. The
photograph of Pu'u Kukui Rainforest Preserve
on p. 35 is courtesy Kapalua Land Company.

PROJECT MANAGER: VIRGINIA WAGEMAN
DESIGNED BY JIM WAGEMAN

*S*unset paints a
pretty backdrop
against the stark
silhouette of
kiawe trees at
Wailea Point.

Contents

Welcome
TO MAUI

"Maui no ka 'oi," residents like to say. "Maui is the best." It's hard to argue with that; the Valley Island is indeed a place of exceptional beauty and vitality.

When seen from the air, it resembles a human head, neck, and torso. The island is actually two dormant volcanoes—Pu'u Kukui (the "head"), the highest peak of the West Maui Mountains, to the west and Haleakalā (the "torso") to the east—joined by a low, flat isthmus (the "neck").

Scientists say these immense land masses were born as separate seamounts on the floor of the Pacific Ocean. Underwater eruptions continued for countless millennia, and the submarine mountains grew bigger and bigger, taller and taller, until they finally emerged above the undulating waves. Subsequent lava flows eventually fused the two volcanoes into one tropical paradise.

Ancient oral history shares a far more romantic tale about Maui's beginnings. One day, so the story goes, Māui, a demigod, decided to go fishing with his brothers. This was to be no ordinary expedition, for Māui took along one of his mother's sacred 'alae birds as bait and a magic fishhook made from the jawbone of an ancestress.

The road to Hāna presents a spectrum of fabulous views, including this one of Honomanū Bay.

High atop Haleakalā Volcano, these visitors are at eye level with the clouds.

Māui and his brothers paddled far out to sea in their canoe, to a site the demigod promised would be abundant with fish. He dropped his line in the water, with the *'alae* firmly fastened on the hook. Down, down, down the line went, to the very bottom of the sea where Pīmoe, a demigod in the guise of an *ulua* fish, kept a tight grip on several bodies of land. When he saw the plump *'alae* dangling before him, the greedy Pīmoe snapped the bird up, hook and all.

Māui felt a strong tug on his line and immediately instructed his brothers to paddle as fast and as hard as they could because he had caught a huge fish. He warned them not to look back or the fish would be lost. One brother, however, could not suppress his curiosity and turned to peek at Māui's incredible catch. What he saw were all the islands of Hawai'i being pulled along with Pīmoe on Māui's fishing line.

In an instant the spell was broken, and the hook slipped out of Pīmoe's mouth. The islands fell into the sea and started drifting away. Pīmoe frantically swam after them and managed to anchor them where they stand today.

Maui's real-life stories are as enthralling as its legends. Three-quarters of its land area is uninhabited wilderness, including Haleakalā National Park, which stretches some twenty-eight thousand acres from the barren summit of the volcano, down its southeastern slope to the verdant Kīpahulu coast. Haleakalā's crater so closely mirrors the moon's surface, American astronauts have trained there for lunar landings.

In 1802 Kamehameha the Great named Lahaina the capital of the Hawaiian

Magnificently, heroically, the rare silversword blooms only once, then dies.

FACING PAGE:
Dawn slips a cloak of pink and lavender over Ālau Island, near Hāna.

kingdom, and so it remained until 1850 when Kamehameha III moved the government seat to Honolulu. The lusty port also won distinction as the center of the whaling industry in the mid-nineteenth century, with a record four hundred ships calling in 1846. There never was a dull day in town, as irreverent sailors clashed head-on with puritanical New England missionaries. Herman Melville, one of the young whalers who visited Lahaina, immortalized the colorful era in his epic novel *Moby Dick*, published in 1851.

The tranquil east coast hamlet of Hāna is cloaked in a thousand shades of green. It is a place where the people are as gentle as the breezes, and the beauty of the land is more astounding than anything man has created of concrete, steel, and glass. Hāna soothes. Hāna calms. Hāna heals. It has provided the perfect retreat for those escaping the hubbub of everyday life, including celebrities such as Carol Burnett, James Garner, Richard Pryor, George Harrison, Jim Nabors, and Kris Kristofferson.

Meticulously fashioned from scrubland, the luxurious resorts of Wailea, Kāʻanapali, and Kapalua host more than two million visitors each year. Their swank properties boast state-of-the-art spas, valuable collections of artwork, award-winning restaurants, and magnificent landscaping—all designed to appeal to the most discriminating of travelers.

Pristine forests and valleys, precious history, posh hotels—it's rare that a place can be all things to all people, but that precisely is the magic of Maui.

West Maui

OF SAILORS, MISSIONARIES, AND KINGS

On the southern side of the area that is now Kā'anapali resort there once was a cave called Ke Ana Pueo, the Owl Cave. Here lived guardian spirits who took the form of rare white Hawaiian pueo (owls).

One morning, a boy named Kā'ili was playing on the beach near his village in Kā'anapali when a group of warriors paddled by in their canoe. They were searching for a sacrifice to appease the war god at Halulu-ko'ako'a Heiau, a place of worship that stood on the coast between Kā'anapali and Lahaina. Being alone and unsupervised, Kā'ili was an easy target; the warriors went ashore and kidnapped him.

Hiding in a nearby grove of coconut palms, Kā'ili's sister, Na'ilima, watched in horror as the warriors headed out to sea with her brother held captive. She ran along the coast, following their canoe until it reached

The charming seaport of Lahaina rests in the shadows of the magnificent West Maui Mountains, close to where Halulu-ko'ako'a Heiau was located. In the mid-1800s it was the hub of whaling activities in the Pacific. As many as fifty ships a day were anchored in its roadstead, and rowdy sailors on leave descended with reckless abandon on the town that devout New England missionaries were trying desperately to tame.

Lahaina still exudes a lively spirit. Nestled amid wonderful boutiques, restaurants, and art galleries are vivid reminders of the town's colorful past, including an authentic replica of a nineteenth-century brig, a wooden prison dating back to 1852, and a museum that once was the residence of Dr.

Halulu-koʻakoʻa. There Naʻilima saw the warriors tie Kāʻili to a sacrificial stone; when dawn came, she knew he would be killed.

Not knowing what to do, Naʻilima ran partway back up the coast. Out of breath and very worried about her brother, she sat in front of a small cave, the Owl Cave, and began to cry. Wahine Peʻe, one of the pueo *who lived there, heard the girl sobbing and came out to see what was wrong. When Naʻilima explained what had happened, Wahine Peʻe promised to help.*

The owl flew to the heiau *and freed Kāʻili. She told him that the warriors would soon discover he had escaped and that he had to outwit them. The way to do this, Wahine Peʻe continued, was to walk backward so that his footprints would appear to lead toward the stone platform of the* heiau, *not away from it.*

Kāʻili followed Wahine Peʻe's instructions and was reunited with Naʻilima at the Owl Cave. The owl then took the children to a hiding place atop Puʻu Kekaʻa, a dark promontory at the northern end of Kāʻanapali that's now popularly known as Black Rock.

By this time the warriors had noticed Kāʻili was missing and immediately set out to recapture him. They found his footprints and followed them—straight back to the heiau! *Wahine Peʻe's plan to thwart them had worked. Later, when it was safe to travel, Kāʻili and Naʻilima returned to their village, their hearts full of gratitude for Wahine Peʻe, their wise and clever* ʻaumakua *(family god).*

A torch-lighting ceremony precedes this diver's dramatic leap off Black Rock in Kāʻanapali.

*M*olokaʻi floats peacefully on an azure cushion, about nine miles from this scenic spot in Kapalua.

Dwight Baldwin, a revered missionary who was the first Western physician in Hawaiʻi. In short, Lahaina is a great place to wander.

The neighboring resorts of Kāʻanapali and Kapalua embrace gorgeous strands of sand. Sailing, snorkeling, swimming, surfing, ocean kayaking, boogie boarding, fishing, whale watching—every day is a pleasure-packed gift for sun lovers.

At twilight each day, a lone youth climbs Black Rock to demonstrate the ancient sport of *lele kawa*, leaping from 300- to 400-foot cliffs into the ocean.

Kahekili, the last king of Maui, excelled at *lele kawa* and is said to have made his most impressive dives from Black Rock.

In olden times Black Rock was regarded as an *'uhane lele*, a sacred place where the souls of the dead jumped into their ancestral spirit land. Kahekili's leaps from this bluff always amazed onlookers not so much because of its height, but because they believed only a person of exceptional spiritual strength could enter the netherworld and escape unharmed.

Indeed, even though it lasts only a few moments, the dive off Black Rock today is mesmerizing. One imagines it is the strong, fearless Kahekili himself who plunges into the sea, his lithe body dramatically silhouetted against a blazing sky.

A daring pilot flies his replica of a 1935 Waco biplane over Kahakuloa Head on Maui's rugged northern coast.

*W*aves batter barren Mōke'ehia islet near Kahakuloa.

FAR LEFT:

*T*he little village of Kahakuloa is the lone sign of civilization in this remote region of West Maui.

*K*ayakers test their courage and skill as they explore the coastline near Mōke'ehia islet.

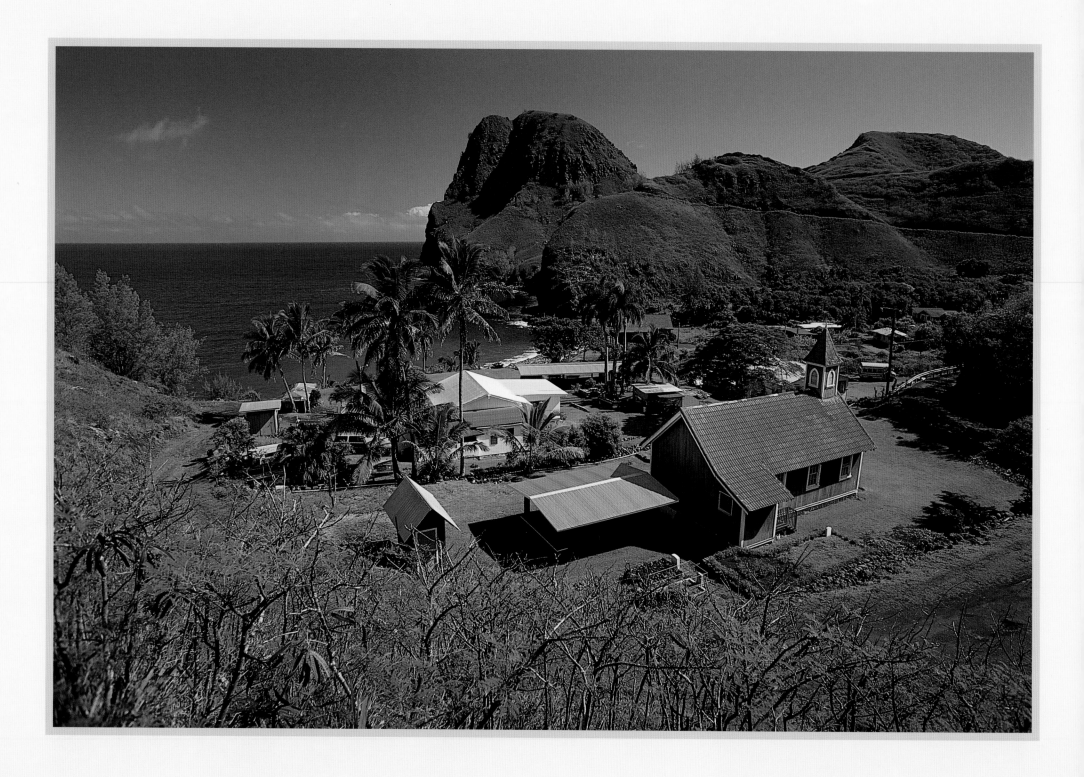

FACING PAGE:

*S*et apart from
the rest of Maui
by craggy hills and
miles of wilderness,
Kahakuloa recalls
the Hawaiʻi of
yesteryear.

*A*s in the old
days, taro patches
flourish in Kaha-
kuloa, whose soil
is nurtured by
frequent rains.

*S*lender palms sway to the gentle rhythm of trade winds at Honolua.

*S*unrise imbues Honolua Bay with an ethereal beauty.

*I*f the arms of Honolua Bay could be extended, they would touch the eastern shore of neighboring Moloka'i.

*S*een from Kapalua, Moloka'i is framed by white clouds, bright pink bougainvillea, and the deep blue of the Pailolo Channel.

The majestic West
Maui Mountains
keep a watchful eye
on the activity in
Lahaina Harbor.

The sails on these
boats moored off
Lahaina will be
hoisted for a day
of snorkeling,
diving, and—
from December
through April—
whale watching.

Carthaginian II is a replica of the type of vessel that carried the first New England missionaries to Hawaiʻi in 1820. A link from its anchor chain is pictured below.

Opened in 1901, Pioneer Inn, with its distinctive red roof, offers commanding views of the harbor and streets of Lahaina.

FACING PAGE,
CLOCKWISE FROM
TOP LEFT:

*B*uilt in 1852, Hale Pa'ahao (stuck-in-irons house) was used to confine sailors accused of desertion, drunkenness, or reckless horseback riding.

*T*he Baldwin Home Museum provides a valuable glimpse of nineteenth-century missionary life.

*C*rumbling walls are all that remain of a fort that was built at the height of the whaling era to monitor the ships that packed Lahaina Harbor.

*T*he Sugar Cane Train chugs between Lahaina and Kā'anapali as the conductor "talks story" with the passengers.

*F*ront Street, Lahaina's main artery, takes on a mystical air after dark.

*D*evotees of the Buddhist faith worship at Lahaina Jōdo Mission, a half mile from the heart of Lahaina town.

*W*o Hing Temple was built in 1912 as a social hall for Lahaina's Chinese residents, many of whom worked on neighboring sugar plantations.

FAR LEFT:
*V*erdant Launiupoko
Valley lies in the
embrace of the West
Maui Mountains.

*O*nly once a year,
twelve people
selected by random
drawing are allowed
to hike into the frag-
ile Pu'u Kukui Rain-
forest Preserve.

PAGES 36–37:
*T*he West Maui
Mountains' usually
well-defined ridges
are veiled by clouds
and the soft light
of afternoon.

*M*ist shrouds
the West Maui
Mountains near
Waikapū.

*W*aiting patiently
for the sun to
relinquish its reign,
a new moon
hovers in the sky
at Launiupoko
Park near Lahaina.

Central Maui

WHERE MAUI'S HEART BEATS

Visitors at the Maui Ocean Center, the largest tropical aquarium in the United States, enjoy a 240-degree view of marine life.

Rising 2,250 feet above sea level, 'Īao Needle is a focal point of lush 'Īao Valley State Park.

Beautiful and serene, 'Īao is the most photographed of Maui's many valleys, largely due to its famed "needle," a 2,250-foot-high basaltic pillar that's as plush and green as the steep rock walls that surround it. It's difficult to believe that in 1790, at this very site, Kamehameha I waged one of the bloodiest battles in his campaign to unite the Hawaiian Islands.

After winning control of the eastern sector of Maui, Kamehameha sailed his canoes to Kahului, then marched to Wailuku where Kalanikupule, son of Maui's king, Kahekili, had rallied his forces. The fierce battle began in Wailuku, but Kamehameha's warriors easily pushed Kalanikupule's troops mauka *(toward the mountains) to 'Īao Valley.*

Although they were spirited fighters, the men of Maui were greatly outnumbered and lacked the weaponry to defend themselves against the

The majority of Maui's population is concentrated in the central part of the island. Here, too, are its county seat (Wailuku), its major harbor and airport, and the bulk of its businesses. The last remaining acres of sugar cane on Maui are planted on this isthmus, as is the island's first notable arts facility—the Maui Arts and Cultural Center.

Central Maui packs a lot of punch. At its southernmost point, Mā'alaea Harbor provides a picturesque backdrop for the Maui Ocean Center, the largest tropical aquarium in the United States. Among its sixty-plus exhibits is a 750,000-gallon saltwater tank that visitors walk through to get a marvelous 240-degree view of sharks, manta rays, various fish, and other intriguing marine life found in Hawaiian waters.

A bustling sugar plantation town at the turn of the century, Pā'ia maintains a much more laid-back mood today.

At Kepaniwai Park Heritage Gardens, on the road to 'Īao Valley State Park, arched bridges, meandering pathways, and lovely gardens link structures representing Hawai'i's many cultural groups. This one is a replica of a Chinese countryside pavilion.

cannon and guns that Kamehameha's haole (foreign) supporters had provided him. They fought valiantly but were driven deeper and deeper into the valley.

Realizing there was no chance for a victory, Kalanikupule and his chiefs managed to flee through a mountain pass, but their courageous soldiers met their demise at the foot of 'Īao Needle. So many bodies fell into 'Īao Stream, they supposedly blocked its usually rapid flow; in fact, this battle became known as Kepaniwai, meaning "the damming of the waters."

Today, a lovely garden at the entrance to 'Īao Valley carries the name Kepaniwai. Tree-lined paths meander past a thatched Hawaiian hale (house), a Japanese teahouse, a Chinese pagoda, and a New England saltbox, all of which pay tribute to the Islands' multiethnic heritage.

Just south of the Ocean Center, the seven-hundred-acre Keālia Pond National Wildlife Preserve harbors a host of waterbirds and shorebirds, including Hawaiian stilts, coots, and ducks; sanderlings; Pacific golden plovers; turnstones; and tattlers. Stealthy photographers have been rewarded with prize images, but be aware—so still is it at this pristine marsh, timid subjects have been known to flee after a single click of a camera's shutter.

To the north, sleepy Pā'ia appears to be the antithesis of its name, which means "noisy." But in the early 1900s the town was just that—a bustling sugar plantation community complete with a school, churches, hospital, bakery, barber and tailor shops, grocery stores, restaurants, and even an acupuncture clinic and piggery. Plantation workers lived in "camps" divided by ethnic groups—Japanese,

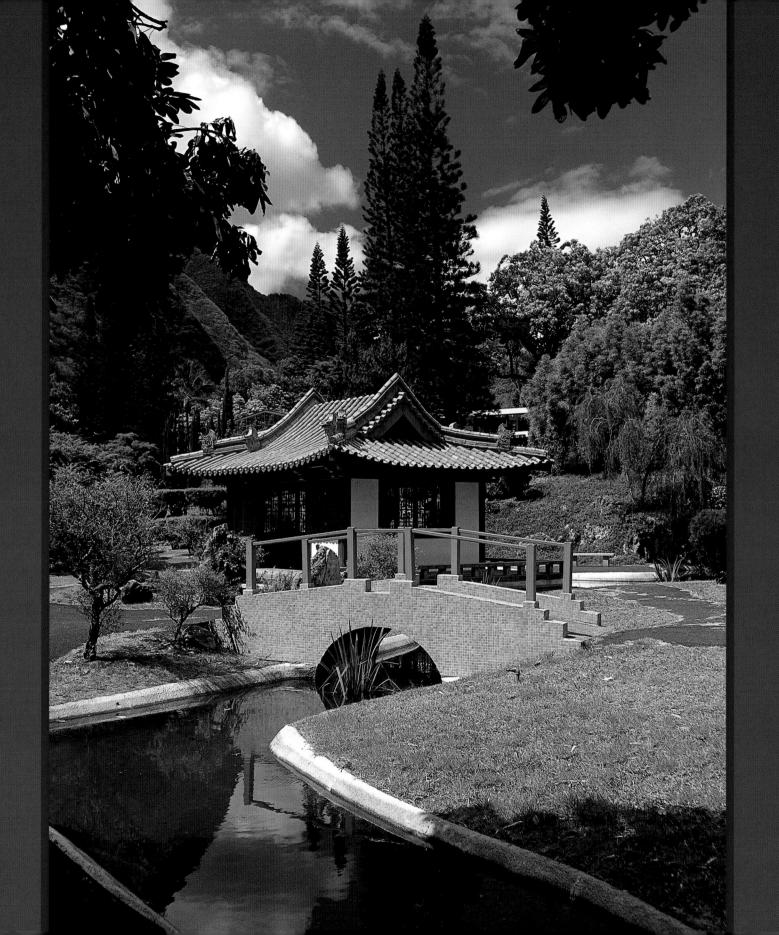

Filipino, Hawaiian, Portuguese, Caucasian. During the 1930s Pā'ia's population of over ten thousand was the largest on Maui.

When sugar production waned and camps started closing in the fifties and sixties, hundreds of Pā'ia Plantation laborers left, lured by the promise of jobs and homes in Kahului, the new "dream city." For two decades Pā'ia languished. Revitalized in the 1980s, the town is now a delightful surprise for passing tourists who take the time to stroll its streets. Unpretentious at first glance, it offers everything from fine art to chic fashions to possibly the best cappuccino this side of Italy.

Brisk winds always bring the best board sailors to Ho'okipa Beach, a ten-minute drive east of Pā'ia, which has been deemed the Aspen of windsurfing. From the shore, these agile athletes look like brightly colored butterflies darting here and there before spinning and somersaulting in a daring flirtation with the waves.

*T*he Maui Arts and Cultural Center in Kahului is the island's premier venue for presentations of the performing and visual arts.

A windsurfer flirts with the waves at Ho'okipa Beach.

*S*hown here from the air, Pā'ia is the last major town travelers hit before embarking on the arduous road to Hāna.

The Maui Ocean Center features more than sixty exhibits, including a touch pool and a 750,000-gallon saltwater tank that's home to nearly two thousand fish, sharks, turtles, stingrays, and other fascinating creatures.

PAGES 48–49:
Expansive lawns, fertile fields, and blooming flowers and fruit trees infuse Maui Tropical Plantation's 120 acres with wonderful colors and scents.

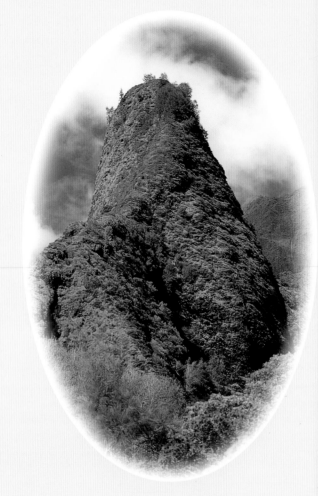

*I*maginative minds could dream up many explanations for ʻĪao Needle's intriguing shape, but the real story is quite simple. Eons of rain and wind eroded the exterior layers of a stone formation, leaving the basaltic spire we see today.

*B*uilt in 1876, Ka'ahumanu Church in Wailuku was named after Queen Ka'ahumanu, Kamehameha I's favorite wife, who was an early convert to Christianity.

*T*he former residence of missionary and sugar planter Edward Bailey, the Bailey House Museum harbors a trove of treasures such as tapa, koa calabashes, and stone adzes.

*K*anahā (left) and Spreckelsville beaches are popular for swimming, sunning, and windsurfing.

FACING PAGE:

*E*ven with
modern machinery
facilitating the
process, planting
and harvesting cane
remain hard work.

*W*ith cane no
longer king,
Puʻunēnē Sugar
Mill is one of
only a few
processing plants
still in operation
in Hawaiʻi.

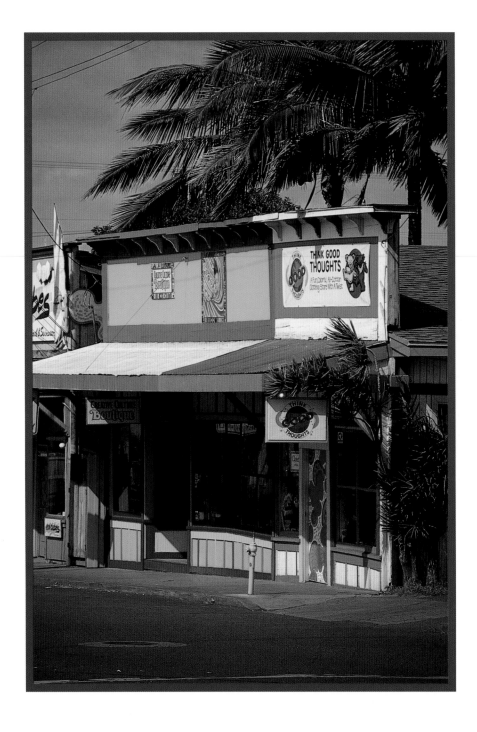

*O*ld storefronts
harking back to
the turn of the
century give Pāʻia
a nostalgic appeal.

PAGES 60–61:
*M*onstrous swells
at Hoʻokipa Beach
provide adrenaline-
pumping challenges
for intrepid wave
riders.

South Maui

A beautiful stranger once visited a seaside fishing village where a handsome young man caught her eye. She approached him and flirted with him, hoping to convince him to come away with her. But the young man's heart belonged to another, and he discouraged her advances, choosing instead to remain at his sweetheart's side.

Furious at being rejected, the stranger then revealed herself as Pele, the volcano goddess. She caused molten lava to fountain from gashes in the earth and began hurling fireballs at the young man who had spurned her. He fled toward the mountains, with Pele literally in hot pursuit.

Observing the chase, the gods took pity on the youth and decided to help him. They turned him into the naupaka kuahiwi, *the mountain* naupaka, *whose fragile snowy petals seem to form only half a flower.*

Look westward from Big Beach in Mākena and you'll see the uninhabited island of Kahoʻolawe anchored on the horizon.

The sunny resort area of Wailea wraps around some of the best beaches in Hawaiʻi.

South Maui basks in the golden glow of sunshine virtually year round. Strung along the warm, dry coast from Kīhei to Mākena are more than a dozen fine beaches and a full range of accommodations, from quaint, cozy bed-and-breakfasts to luxurious resorts whose top-of-the-line suites go for up to ten thousand dollars per night.

Sculpted from fifteen hundred acres of *kiawe* brush and rugged lava, Wailea resort is the jewel of South Maui. Its multimillion-dollar hotels hug the ocean and five gorgeous crescents of white sand. Travelers seeking the perfect tropical escape just might find it here.

Wailea means "waters of Lea," the Hawaiian god-

This made Pele angrier, and she next turned her attention to the frightened maiden. The fiery goddess summoned a flow of hot lava and used it to chase the girl down to the ocean. Just when Pele had her cornered, the gods intervened and transformed her into the naupaka kahakai, *the beach* naupaka, *which blankets the shoreline at Wailea. Its delicate white flowers also look as though they've been torn in half.*

Blooming far apart from each other, the naupaka kuahiwi *and the* naupaka kahakai *recall the tragic young lovers who were forever separated by the wrath of Hawai'i's volcano goddess.*

dess of canoe makers. Lea was able to transform herself into the **'elepaio** bird and would fly alongside canoe builders as they roamed the forest in search of sound logs. If the **'elepaio** walked the entire length of a log without stopping, the wood was solid. If the bird paused and pecked for insects, the log was decaying inside and would not be seaworthy.

Beyond manicured, sophisticated Wailea, the ambience suddenly changes. You're engulfed by wilderness and a feeling of solitude. The beauty is still there—it's just raw, natural, pristine.

Two imposing landmarks in the area are linked by a legend. Pele, the volcano goddess, once loved a mortal named Lohi'au, who took a *mo'o* (dragon) as his wife. In a jealous fit, Pele cut the *mo'o* in half. Her head became Pu'u Ōla'i, a cinder cone along the shore, and her tail splashed into the sea as a sliver of an islet known as Molokini.

In 1786, French explorer Jean François de Galaup, known as the Comte de La Pérouse, anchored his ships in a nearby bay and earned a place in Hawaiian history as the first European to set foot on Maui. In his journal, La Pérouse noted the "burning climate" of the southern coast, which proved to be eerily prophetic. Four years after his visit, Haleakalā erupted, sending rivers of molten lava down its flanks in a fiery path to the Pacific. The majestic mountain has been slumbering ever since.

With clear, calm waters that deepen gradually, Wailea Beach (below) is a wonderful choice for swimmers. A couple strolls along pristine Wailea Point (right), which is hemmed by ebony lava.

Ulua Beach (facing page) is one of five cream-colored crescents that adorn the resort area of Wailea.

*I*n Mākena, a 360-foot cinder cone named Puʻu Ōlaʻi separates Oneloa or Big Beach (right) and Little Beach, also named Puʻu Ōlaʻi. Cinder cones are hills formed by the accumulation of volcanic debris.

*B*ig Beach, whose Hawaiian name means "long sand," measures 3,300 feet long and over 100 feet wide.

*E*ven the most steadfast landlubbers have to admit there's something grand, something truly adventurous, about setting out to sea. Concierges at Wailea's resorts can book sailing expeditions that fit every time frame and budget.

*M*aui satiates the avid water lover. 'Āhihi-Kīna'u Natural Area Reserve (left, top and bottom) is perfect for kayaking and snorkeling.

*W*ith dramatic coral reefs and myriad fish, Molokini islet (below and facing page, top) is one of the state's best snorkeling sites.

A couple dives with the turtles off Mākena Landing (facing page, bottom left), and a hump-back whale and her calf cruise the South Maui waters (facing page, bottom right).

Upcountry Maui
TOWARD THE HOUSE OF THE SUN

In a scene reminiscent of a Hollywood Western, horses roam verdant pastureland at 'Ulupalakua Ranch.

Exploding in a brilliant burst of light at the summit of Haleakalā, sunrise signals the start of a new day.

The people of Maui were unhappy. The sun traveled so swiftly across the sky they couldn't get their work done, let alone have time for recreation. Fishermen paddled out to their favorite fishing spots, but before they could pull in a decent catch, night would fall. Farmers planted, weeded, and harvested crops in their fields, but darkness swept in before they could finish their tasks. The village women were frustrated because the sun did not linger long enough to dry their newly made sheets of kapa *(tapa).*

"You must ask the sun to go more slowly," the goddess Hina begged her son, the demigod Māui. "How else can we complete our chores?" Māui promised to help.

For several days he observed the sun's path. Each morning it arrived through an opening in the crater of the massive volcano named

Local people call the fertile belt that wraps around the midriff of Haleakalā Crater "Upcountry." Here, at a cool three to four thousand feet above sea level, farmers tend flourishing fields of carnations, roses, proteas, cabbages, and onions so sweet they can be eaten raw. Carnelian grapes thrive on twenty-two acres at 'Ulupalakua Ranch, whose Tedeschi Vineyards label has become known worldwide. In addition to libations produced from these grapes, Tedeschi offers a crisp pineapple wine called Maui Blanc and a zesty pineapple–passion fruit wine dubbed Maui Splash.

Upcountry also is the center of ranching on Maui.

Haleakalā (house of the sun) and then drifted up into the sky. "Perfect!" Māui thought. "That is where I can snare the sun and force it to move more slowly."

The akamai (smart) demigod gathered a pile of coconut fibers and twisted them into a strong rope. Carrying the rope and his war club, he began climbing up the mountain. Higher and higher he went, until he reached a cave on Haleakalā's slopes. There he waited until he saw the very first ray, or leg, of sunlight burst through the opening in the crater.

Māui threw his rope and lassoed that leg. Unable to move, the sun called out irritably, "Who is holding on to my leg? Let go of it at once!"

"It is I, Māui," the demigod replied, "and I refuse to release you until you promise to move more slowly across the sky so my people will have more light and warmth to work and play."

Native to Australia and South Africa, proteas thrive between the 2,000- and 4,000-foot elevations of Haleakalā, which provide ideal growing conditions —warm days; cool nights; rich, well-drained soil; and protective cloud cover. The flower pictured here is a king protea.

Cattle and horses graze contentedly on ranch land near Makawao.

It's not unusual to see *paniolo* (cowboys) trotting their horses down Makawao's main street, but don't let this fool you; Makawao is definitely not a cow town. Tucked behind its rustic storefronts are trendy art galleries, restaurants, and clothing boutiques.

Haleakalā National Park is Maui's biggest playground. Three thousand feet deep, with a circumference of twenty-one miles, the volcano's enormous crater could contain the entire island of Manhattan, skyscrapers and all. Active travelers can indulge in camping, hiking, biking, and horseback riding in a spectacular setting that resembles the face of the moon. For many, a visit to Haleakalā begins at its 10,023-foot-high summit,

The sun replied, "I will not make that promise to you!" By now, more of its legs were appearing through the opening in the crater. Māui struck the leg he had been holding with his club and broke it off. Then he slipped his rope around another leg and grasped it tightly.

"Will you promise to slow your speed?" Māui asked.

The sun remained defiant. "No!"

Māui again broke the leg he was holding, and as other legs appeared, he broke the strongest of those too. Weakened, the sun finally agreed to compromise. For half the year, spring and summer, it consented to remain in the sky longer so the people could fish, dry their kapa, *and work in the fields. During the other half of the year, fall and winter, it would journey through the sky more quickly. And so this arrangement has remained to this day.*

where each day possibly the best show in the Islands is staged—sunrise.

Lofty Haleakalā is the only place on Maui where the rare silversword plant grows. A cousin of the common sunflower, the silversword attains a kingly height of seven feet in its five- to twenty-year life span, but that's not its most remarkable trait. In what is surely one of nature's most bizarre and bittersweet performances, it blooms only once before dying, transforming its spindly stalk into a glorious display of up to five hundred flowers ranging in color from pale yellow to purplish red.

*L*ooking like a set from "Bonanza," Makawao fits perfectly into Upcountry's rustic lifestyle.

*T*rendy clothing boutiques and art galleries are housed behind many of the town's humble wooden storefronts.

*C*rowds jam Makawao's main street each year to watch the festive Fourth of July parade.

*M*akawao's Fourth of July celebration culminates in a rodeo that draws the best cowboys in the state. Spectators cheer their favorites in thrilling events such as bronco busting and calf roping.

*J*ust outside of Makawao, Hui No'eau Visual Arts Center offers art classes, demonstrations, exhibitions, and a noteworthy gift shop. Originally the home of prominent Maui residents Harry and Ethel Baldwin, the Mediterranean-style villa was built in 1917.

*T*his breathtaking late afternoon view from 'Ulu-palakua looks toward the West Maui Mountains.

*P*roteas, lettuce, cabbage, and strawberries are among the bountiful crops raised at Upcountry farms.

FACING PAGE:

*B*efore yielding to night, the sun casts its final rays on a field of vanda orchids.

*B*looming jacaranda trees brighten the grounds of Holy Ghost Catholic Church in Kula.

With the world's largest dormant volcano as its centerpiece, Haleakalā National Park sprawls over 28,655 geologically diverse acres. Haleakalā Volcano's massive crater—an otherworldly montage of cinder cones, lava flows, and mini craters—is 7.5 miles long, 2.5 miles wide, 3,000 feet deep, and 21 miles in circumference.

PAGES 96–97:
*H*aleakalā Crater is awesome in both size and appearance.

*P*ark boundaries stretch from sea level to Haleakalā's 10,023-foot-high summit. In between is an amazing variety of climates and terrain, including rain-soaked forests, fertile fields, and barren desert. Thirty-six miles of hiking trails crisscross the crater and flanks of Haleakalā. Other diversions include biking, camping, and horseback riding.

East Maui

HEAVEN ON EARTH

A fisherman named Kū'ula lived with his wife Hina and son 'Ai'ai in Hāna. Kū'ula never had trouble catching fish; they came readily to his hooks, nets, and traps as if they were drawn by magnets. When his neighbors were less fortunate, Kū'ula always shared the bounty he had harvested. He even built a fishpond by the sea and filled it with every kind of fish imaginable.

Stories about Kū'ula's skill as a fisherman circulated throughout the island and caught the attention of the high chief of Maui. He appointed Kū'ula head fisherman, and the amiable man from Hāna served the chief faithfully for many years.

Then trouble began. For some reason, fish started disappearing from Kū'ula's once well-stocked pond. Night after night, the supply dwindled, causing the fisherman great concern. One evening, he decided to stand guard at the pond to see if he could catch the culprit red-handed.

The night passed without incident, then at daybreak Kū'ula saw an

Heaven lies at the end of a road from hell. That's how Mauians jokingly describe the journey to Hāna, which many regard as the most beautiful place in the Islands. The drive is long (fifty-two miles from Kahului Airport) and grueling (fifty-six one-lane bridges must be crossed and 617 twists and turns—12 per mile—must be negotiated). Without taking a break, the trip can be completed in about three hours. Wisely, most people take all day, making plenty of stops for photos. The images that unfold along the way are truly astounding—hills and ravines draped in a mantle of brilliant green; cobalt blue surf pounding stoic crags; waterfalls cascading into cool, clear pools; a luscious array of fruits and flowers in perpetual bloom. Seventeen miles from Hāna, Ke'anae Peninsula

enormous eel slither through the gate and into his pond. So this was the creature that was eating his fish! "This cunning eel lives in a cave on the windward side of Moloka'i," a neighbor told Kū'ula. "He is worshiped by the people there."

"That doesn't matter," the perturbed fisherman said. "He's stealing my fish, and that must stop."

Kū'ula assigned his son the task of going to the island of Moloka'i and getting rid of the monster eel, and that 'Ai'ai did. When word spread that the eel had been killed at the hands of a youth from Hāna, the people of Moloka'i were outraged. One man plotted revenge. He moved to Maui and became a trusted servant of the high chief. It was not long before he began whispering lies about Kū'ula to the chief.

Angered by what he heard, the chief forgot that Kū'ula had been a faithful retainer and sentenced him and his family to death. Soldiers rushed to Kū'ula's house, tied the three to posts, and set the thatch ablaze. As flames burned hot and bright, smoke rose and the spirits of Kū'ula and Hina drifted with it to the sea. Meanwhile, Ai'ai was able to undo the cords that bound him, and, with thick smoke providing cover, he escaped to the mountains.

Living incognito, the youth taught villagers there lessons he had learned from his father. He showed them how to weave fish traps from

juts out from the coastline, snug and secure beneath a patchwork of taro. It seems nature chose the most vivid colors on her palette to paint these scenes.

Hāna itself drowses in alternating sunshine and showers. It has no fast-food outlets, theaters, shopping malls, nightclubs, or video game parlors. Every day the mood is peaceful, the pace deliberate—Sunday distinguishable only by the joyous outpouring of hymns from the town's two churches.

Avid beachgoers have their choice of colors in East Maui: ebony Pa'iloa in Wai'ānapanapa State Park (this picturesque pocket of black shingle is nice for sunbathing, not for swimming); the rust red of remote Kaihalulu (created by volcanic cinders, it's the only red sand beach in Hawai'i and one of only a few in the world); the deep brown of Kapueokahi (the safest swimming beach in this sector of the island); and the rich cream of crescent-shaped Hāmoa, which novelist James Michener described as "so perfectly formed that I wonder at its comparative obscurity."

morning glory vines and advised them to pray before launching their canoes so the gods would protect them and reward them with a sizable catch. He also instructed them to build shrines along the shore—sometimes they were simply piles of stones, other times they were images sculpted in the likeness of a man. Here fishermen placed offerings of leis and the first fish they caught on every trip.

These shrines can be seen today on every island. They are called kū'ula in honor of the fisherman from Hāna who is now revered as the Hawaiian god of fishermen.

This simple stone plaque in the cemetery of Palapala Ho'omau Church in Kīpahulu marks the final resting place of famed aviator Charles Lindbergh.

In Kīpahulu, ten misty miles beyond Hāna, a series of fern-fringed plunge pools descends gracefully seaward. Part of 'Ohe'o Stream, they were nicknamed the "Seven Sacred Pools" in the late forties by an enthusiastic public relations executive, but there are actually two dozen pools, not seven, and although the area is certainly beautiful, it is not considered sacred. The misleading moniker has endured over the decades, but *kama'āina* (longtime Island residents) rightfully discourage it, preferring the spot's correct name, 'Ohe'o Gulch, be used. Heavy rains make the pools dangerous during the winter, but in the calm of summer they are a divine place for a dip.

Aviator Charles Lindbergh chose to be buried in Kīpahulu, far from the glaring spotlight that enveloped him for most of his life. Marked only by a quilt of *'ili'ili* (small stones) and a slab of weather-worn granite, his grave in the cemetery of Palapala Ho'omau Church reflects the sublime simplicity of East Maui.

*S*pectacular panoramas can be admired all along the road to Hāna.

*S*ilvery waterfalls often pierce the area's deep green raiment.

*B*ecause flowers grow in great abundance here, you can buy a bucketful of blooms at very reasonable prices.

Construction of Piʻilanihale Heiau, the largest ancient Hawaiian place of worship in existence, was completed in the sixteenth century. Named for Piʻilani, one of Maui's great chiefs, its terraced stone platform measures 415 feet long by 340 feet wide.

Black sand beaches at Waiʻānapanapa complement the rich green of the landscape.

The hamlet of
Hāna lies at Maui's
easternmost point.

After conquering
the "road from
hell," visitors reward
themselves with a
refreshing shave ice.

*T*he Hasegawa General Store sells everything from door hinges to dog collars.

PAGES 112–113: *H*āna highlights include Kaihalulu, the only red sand beach in Hawai'i; Blue Pool, which is fed by a 100-foot waterfall; and lovely Hāna Bay, basking here in the glow of sunrise.

ʻĀlau Island, located
a quarter-mile off
Kōkī Beach, is pro-
tected by the state of
Hawaiʻi as a seabird
sanctuary.

One of Hāna's best
beaches, Hāmoa is a
popular playground
for experienced
swimmers, surfers,
and bodysurfers.

*D*ense greenery
engulfs Wailua Falls.

*Q*uaint Saint
Gabriel's Church,
dating from 1870,
welcomes
worshipers in
Wailua, just off
the Hāna Highway.

*M*aui's eastern coast remains magnificent wilderness.

*I*n remote
Kaupō, those who
constructed Hui
Aloha Church seem
to have purposely
kept its design
simple so as not
to detract from
the splendor of
its surroundings.

*O*n a clear day,
you can see the
northern tip of the
Big Island from
Maui's eastern shore.

References

Belknap, Jodi Parry. *Kaanapali.* Honolulu: Amfac Property Corporation, 1981.

Bisignani, J. D. *Hawaii Handbook: The All-Island Guide.* Chico, Calif.: Moon Publications, 1995.

Clark, John. *The Beaches of Maui County.* Honolulu: University of Hawai'i Press, 1989.

Fornander, Abraham. *Ancient History of the Hawaiian People.* 1880. Honolulu: Mutual Publishing, 1996.

Foster, Jeanette, and Jocelyn Fujii. *Frommer's '99 Hawaii.* New York: Simon and Schuster, 1998.

Knipe, Rita. *The Water of Life: A Jungian Journey through Hawaiian Myth.* Honolulu: University of Hawai'i Press, 1989.

Lee, Robin Koma. *Legends of the Hawaiian Rain Forest.* Honolulu: Makapu'u Press, 1980.

Pūku'i, Mary Kawena, comp. *Tales of the Menehune.* Honolulu: Kamehameha Schools Bernice Pauahi Bishop Estate, 1994.

———. *The Water of Kāne and Other Legends of the Hawaiian Islands.* Honolulu: Kamehameha Schools Bernice Pauahi Bishop Estate, 1994.

Stames, C. Alexander. *Hawaiian Folklore Tales.* Hicksville, N.Y.: Exposition Press, 1975.

Tregaskis, Moana. *Hawai'i.* Oakland, Calif.: Compass American Guides, 1998.